Zebras
For Kids

Amazing Animal Books
For Young Readers

By
Rachel Smith

Mendon Cottage Books
JD-Biz Corp Publishing

Read More Amazing Animal Books

Table of Contents

Introduction

The zebra is one crazy-looking animal; it's covered in stripes, and that's not something you see in a lot of animals. Tigers, okapis, tabby cats... the list is not incredibly long.

Since the beginning, zebras have fascinated Westerners. Africans lived with them for a long time, so they were not a surprise to them, but to the Westerner, a striped animal was an oddity to be marveled at and taken home for other people to gawk at. In some ways, it's still this way.

The zebra, a relative of the horse and donkey, has never been domesticated. It probably never will be.

What are zebras?

A zebra belongs to the genus Equus, which horses and donkeys also belong to, among other creatures. However, the subgenera that zebras belong to include Hippotigris and Dolichohippus. The thing that unites zebras as a type of animal is the stripes that go up and down their bodies.

Drinking zebras.

Some people have described the zebra as a striped horse. There is some truth in that description, but zebras have their differences.

Zebras are slower than horses in general. However, they do have a very good stamina, which really helps in outrunning predators.

Two of the kinds of zebras are more related to horses, and one kind is more related to donkeys. The main reason they are grouped together is because they are striped.

Another key thing is that, despite having white underbellies, zebras are actually black with white markings. The stripes occur for a number of reasons: to blend in, to dazzle predators, possibly to identify, as every pattern is unique, attracting fewer flies, and possibly even helping with the heat.

Zebras have amazing vision. Scientists even believe they can see in color. They also have very great hearing, and unlike horses and donkeys, they can rotate their ears.

There are also zebras that have cream coloring instead of black, or are completely white. This is sort of rare, but happens enough for it to be considered a fairly common thing.

Zebras are susceptible to various diseases, such as pneumonia and pleuritis. They also sometimes get parasites, such as ticks or botsfly larvae. They can be easily poisoned by red maple tree leaves, the same as horses, ponies, and donkeys.

How do zebras act?

For starters, most types of zebras live in groups called harems. This consists of a male zebra, his mates, up to seven or so, and their babies. It is the male's job to protect his harem. However, some kinds of zebras are more solitary, only coming together to mate, and staying in groups of a mare and her foals and males staying alone. In both groups, however, unmated males often form groups together.

A zebra foal.

The social groups of the latter zebra could best be described as sometimes coming together for a few months, and then breaking up.

They are alone for most of the time, except for when a mother has a foal.

Zebras sleep standing up. This is another thing they have in common with horses. However, they don't usually sleep without first making sure there's an awake zebra in their group to alert them to predators and the like.

They have a few ways of communicating, though it depends on the type of zebra which they use. For instance, high-pitched barks and whinnying are pretty normal for most zebras. However, in a smaller group of zebras, braying, rather like mules, is very normal.

Their ears also indicate things about how they're feeling. If they're straight up, or erect, they are happy. If they're pulled forward, then the zebra is scared. If they are pulled backwards, the zebra is angry. However, they also can have erect ears when they are looking for predators; at the same time, they will stare and hold their head high.

Zebras eat mainly grasses. This doesn't mean they won't eat things like shrubs and other plants; it just means they eat a whopping majority of grasses. Most animals, even other herbivores (plant eaters), can't survive on the diet of a zebra, but a zebra's digestive system is specially designed to make the zebra survive on less nutrition than other animals.

Male zebras don't really help with raising the foals, though they might protect them in certain types of zebras. It's on the mother to feed and rear the foal. In some types, it's entirely on her to protect the foal too.

A female zebra has about one foal a year, though she also nurses each foal for a year. Zebra foals are entirely able to stand, walk, and nurse shortly after birth. This is something else they have in common with horses; it makes sense because a zebra mother certainly can't carry her baby around. Baby zebras are born white and brown instead of white and black.

Zebras and humans

Humans have always wanted to tame zebras and ride them like horses. There was a big push to do this in the late 1800s and early 1900s, and a lot of work was done to try to domesticate them.

Zebras in a zoo.

The main issue with domesticating the zebra is that it's a bit more unpredictable than the horse or donkey, and it tends to panic under stress. For instance, a crowded city would undoubtedly cause it to panic, whereas a horse could be trained to maneuver in such a setting.

Horses have a long history of being bred to carry people, pull loads, and generally be manageable. It's been possibly even thousands of years since the horse was domesticated, and so the ability to be tamed runs in its veins, meaning that it's somewhat genetic.

A zebra has only been trained, in some instances, in the first generation, which is a huge difference between them and the horse.

There are many examples of attempts towards domesticating zebras. One is the zoological collector Walter Rothschild, who managed to get zebras to pull his carriage in England. He was a man back in the late 1800s and early 1900s who collected animals, both alive and as specimens. He had hundreds of thousands of specimens, and hired a librarian, scientists, explorers, and taxidermists (people who stuff animals) to make a vast collection, mostly of birds and butterflies.

Another example is the story of Rosendo Ribeiro, in 1907. He was British and Portuguese, and the first physician in Kenya. He would ride a zebra he'd tamed to make house calls with his patients. Back then, house calls were very normal, and especially in a place like Kenya where people were far apart. He tamed the zebra himself, though whatever his method was, it was never imitated in quite the same way.

The governor, George Grey, originally served in South Africa. There, he acquired some zebras. They were trained to pull his carriage, and when he was made governor of New Zealand in the mid-19th century, he brought them all the way to New Zealand. They would pull his carriage around his private island.

In the piece "Points of the Horse" by Captain Horace Hays in 1893, he goes over different zebra species and the relative difficulty of trying to tame them. He relates taming a zebra stallion in 1891, despite it being a full grown stallion and being intact. He says he 'broke' it and discusses how to 'break' various kinds of zebras. He compares each kind, saying that Burchell's zebra is easy to break and immune to the tsetse fly. The quagga, an extinct kind of zebra (but not extinct at that time), is one he considered best for domestication because it was easy to train to wear a saddle.

These instances aside, zebras have not been able to be consistently domesticated or tamed by anyone. It would probably take a long time to have truly domesticated zebras, and in these instances, the zebra often was not ridden or not exposed to the same stresses as a horse.

Zebras have long been hunted for skins and meat. This has been done both by the native Africans (in various countries and cultural groups) and by the colonists who moved in. They were also hunted to stuff and bring home, or they were also captured to put in zoos. However, wild zebras are not often captured to put in zoos anymore, since they breed well in captivity.

Nowadays, sometimes zebra herds are culled. This means that they hunt zebras and kill them to bring down their numbers; this is done with a lot of abundant animals throughout the world. The problem with leaving them the way they are is that it often causes damage to the environment when there are too many.

However, the zebras that are endangered are never culled this way.

Zebras also show up in African cultures. For example, the San people of Namibia have a tale of how the zebra got its stripes: it fought with a baboon over a watering hole, and because it kicked so hard, it got dizzy and fell on a fire; the stripes are scorch marks.

The Karamojong tribe of Uganda reveres the zebra, and the women will paint themselves with black and white stripes and act like them. It's considered the height of beauty.

Interestingly, the practice of a Tijuana Zebra is performed in Tijuana, Mexico. It is not a real zebra, but instead a light-colored donkey painted with black stripes. The practice started when photographs were taken in black and white, and the donkeys would look ghostly. So, they painted black stripes on them to make them stand out, and they dubbed them zebras. It was not an attempt to trick anyone, however, as everyone involved knew they were just painted donkeys.

The Tijuana Zebra is part of the tourist culture in Tijuana.

It has also been proven that a bacteria in the zebra's feces (poop) can turn cellulose into butanol fuel. This has not been made into a big thing, but it may be in the future.

What kinds of zebras are there?

There are three main types. The Grévy's zebra, the plains zebra, and the mountain zebra; then there are several subtypes, especially of the plains zebra.

A plains zebra.

The plains zebra, also known as the common zebra, is the most common kind of zebra. It includes the subtypes of: the quagga (which is extinct), Burchell's zebra, Grant's zebra, the maneless zebra,

Chapman's zebra, and Crawshay's zebra. Their patterns can vary greatly, sometimes even including brown stripes among the black.

Then there's the mountain zebra. It has two subtypes, the Hartman's mountain zebra and the Cape mountain zebra. It, unlike its cousin the plains zebra, is endangered to an extent. There is the suggestion that these are actually two separate species, but scientists haven't decided on that yet.

Lastly, there the Grévy's zebra, which is in a different subgenus than the other two. It's also known as the imperial zebra. It is the largest kind of wild equine (horse-type creature).

Beyond that, there are also types of zebra hybrids. The zorse, which is a hybrid of a zebra and a horse; the zonkey, which is a hybrid of a zebra and a donkey; and the zony, which is a cross between a zebra and a pony.

Plains zebra

The plains zebra, or the common zebra, is the one most commonly in zoos. It's not only the most common numerically (by how many there are) but also it is the most widespread geographically speaking. That means that you can find the plains zebra in more different places than any other zebra.

A pair of plains zebras.

And it is a wide range, from the south of Ethiopia in the north to Botswana and eastern South Africa in the south. This is why it is in the Botswana national coat of arms.

The plains zebra is the zebra most like a horse. However, they are often found with Grévy's zebras in areas that they share habitat, and they interbreed with them despite them being more like donkeys. The hybrid babies seem to do well in their herds.

There are several kinds of plains zebras. For one, there's the maneless zebra. It is simply different in that it has a short or no mane. A mane is the hair along the neck of the equine.

Then there's Grant's zebra (which, just to be honest, many of these zebras are named after the people who 'discovered' them, because scientists back then were kind of big-headed). This is the smallest kind of plains zebra. It has vertical stripes in front, horizontal on its back legs, and diagonal on its rump (rear end).

Grant's zebra used to have a wider range than it does now; the problem is that there have been a lot of civil wars and the like in the countries it lives or used to live in, and it's been made regionally extinct, which means it can no longer be found in certain areas, but it still exists.

Chapman's zebra lives in herds of up to tens of thousands, all broken down into small family groups. This type of zebra sometimes doesn't get black stripes after being born with the normal brown stripes. It also sometimes has brown patches on its body. They're not extremely at risk, but they are threatened by the habitat destruction and poaching going on in much of Africa.

The issue with distinguishing different types of subspecies within the plains zebra is that no two zebras' coats are exactly alike. So many different kinds of zebras were reported in the earlier days of exploring Africa for zoology that no one knew just how many types of zebras there really were.

The trick is to find actual differences among a group of the animal. For instance, Crawshay's zebra is different because of its teeth. Others are different due to types of stripes or color variations.

With northern plains zebras, they tend to have narrower stripes. With the southern plains zebras, they tend to have wider stripes and shadow stripes, which are extra brown stripes.

Sometimes, there are albino zebras, though these have really only showed up in Kenya. As mentioned before, cream-colored zebras are a variation, though they are not albinos.

Plains zebras' main predators are lions and spotted hyenas. These will try to take down full grown zebras. Another predator, at least when they're crossing rivers, is the Nile crocodile. Minor predators include wild dogs, cheetahs, and leopards, but they tend to only go after foals. Sometimes, olive baboons will go after foals too.

Plains zebras get along with wildebeests very well, and can peacefully coexist with them. Their herds can easily be mixed together, grazing in the same area, with no problems.

Mountain zebra

Mountain zebras come in two subspecies: the Cape mountain zebra, and Hartmann's mountain zebra. It is a lot less diverse than the plains zebra, and it also far less widespread.

A mountain zebra.

Mountain zebras have a dewlap, which other zebras don't have. They are striped black or dark brown and white, though Hartmann's mountain zebra is more of a buff color than the Cape mountain zebra.

The Cape mountain zebra is sexually dimorphic; that means that the sexes, male and female, are different. In this case, the female is larger than the male.

Both kinds have unbarred bellies, meaning that they have no stripes on their stomachs.

Unsurprisingly, mountain zebras prefer to live in mountainous areas. However, they will live in grassland, wooded areas, and other spots. Their range doesn't really overlap much with the other zebras', though.

They live in hot, dry, and rocky mountainous and hilly areas. They like slopes and plateaus that are really high, such as over a thousand meters above sea level. They prefer to eat tufted grass, but will eat bark, berries, shrubs, and other things when there isn't enough of that.

Cape mountain zebras and Hartmann's mountain zebras are what is called allopatric. This means that, due to deforestation and other habitat destruction, their habitats don't overlap. This means that they don't interbreed, because they never come in contact with each other. They also never come in contact with other kinds of zebras, since most plains zebras and Grévy's zebras prefer flat grassland.

Unlike plains zebras, mountain zebras don't gather in large herds. They have small family groups instead, and their numbers never reach beyond ten, much less the thousands and thousands that a plains zebra herd can have.

Another reason the mountain zebra has a smaller habitat is that there are less of them now. They are in lands that have experienced a lot of violence, and so, they were often hunted for meat. They were also hunted for poachers, and their habitat destruction also led to less food for them to eat.

The Cape mountain zebra is endangered, probably the most endangered kind of zebra.

Grévy's zebra

Grévy's zebra is endangered. It is the most endangered overall species out of any zebra. It's also the largest zebra, and the tallest. It was named after Jules Grévy, the first president of the Third French Republic.

A number of Grévy's zebras.

Grévy's zebra is the one kind of zebra that doesn't form family groups in the same way the other zebras do. Sometimes, these zebras come together for mating and such, but they'll break up within months.

They can survive for five days without water. It lives in a semi-arid area that sometimes overlaps with plains zebra areas.

This zebra was known to the Romans and other groups in antiquity. They used them in circuses, which were a big part of Roman culture at one point. The phrase 'Panem et circenses' was used to describe the ruling powers' way of pacifying (keeping happy) the Roman citizens. This meant 'Bread and circuses' and it meant that they gave them free bread and free circuses to keep them satisfied.

It mainly lives in Ethiopia, and it has been given as a gift by places such as the kingdom of Shoa, which was in central Ethiopia.

There aren't a whole lot of differences physically, besides size and slight differences in coloring, such as a white muzzle.

There are only 3,000 left, though they are stabilizing. The destruction of habitat and hunting has led to its endangerment, but it is now protected by the Ethiopian government.

Quagga

The quagga is a kind of plains zebra that existed in South Africa. It went extinct in 1883.

The main differences between it and other plains zebras was the coloring; it had brown all over it, and stripes in the front and back. There are only 23 skins left, with photographs of only one quagga.

The problem for it was that it lived in areas that the Dutch (who had South Africa at the time, as a colony) wanted to raise livestock and farm in. So, the quagga was mercilessly hunted.

It didn't take long for it to become endangered, but by the time Europe realized what had happened and took steps to try to save it, it was too late.

They tried to breed it in their own zoos, but didn't succeed.

Nowadays, there's a program where they're trying to bring back the quagga through breeding. Only time will tell if this is successful.

Zebroids

Zebroid is the name for any zebra hybrid. There are three main kinds:

The zorse. This is a cross between a female horse and a male zebra. A cross between a male horse and a female zebra is a horbra or a hebra. It's incredibly rare for the latter pairing to happen.

Zorses.

Next is the zony. This is a cross between a female pony and a male zebra. One kind that's used is the Shetland pony, resulting in zetlands.

Last is the zonkey, zebonkey, or zedonk. This is a cross between a male zebra and a female donkey. These are very rare, even though both are related by being in the horse family.

All of these hybrids are infertile, unable to make babies. This is due to genetics, and it's the case with hybrids the world over.

Conclusion

Zebras are a beautiful creature that means a lot to the African cultures it's involved in.

With its many types, and even the hybrids, it's a varied and interesting creature. It's not so well known that the zebra has several kinds, and it's a gem of knowledge that you have now.

Hopefully, the zebra will not go the way of the quagga, and will remain a strong player in its African ecosystems.

Author Bio

Rachel Smith is a young author who enjoys animals. Once, she had a rabbit who was very nervous, and chewed through her leash and tried to escape. She's also had several pet mice, who were the funniest little animals to watch. She lives in Ohio with her family and writes in her spare time.

Publisher

JD-Biz Corp

P O Box 374

Mendon, Utah 84325

http://www.jd-biz.com/

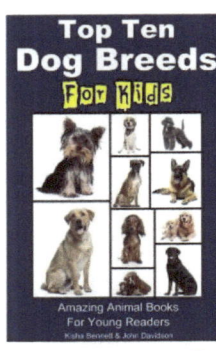

Top Ten Dog Breeds For Kids
Amazing Animal Books For Young Readers
Kisha Bennett & John Davidson

German Shepherds
Dog Books for Kids
K. Bennett

Bulldogs
Dog Books for Kids
K. Bennett

Dachshund
Dog Books for Kids
K. Bennett

Poodles
Dog Books for Kids
K. Bennett

Labrador Retrievers
Dog Books for Kids
K. Bennett

Rottweilers
Dog Books for Kids
K. Bennett

Boxers
Dog Books for Kids
K. Bennett

Puppies
Dog Books For Kids
Amazing Animal Books
By John Davidson

Golden Retrievers
Dog Books for Kids
K. Bennett

Beagles
Dog Books for Kids
K. Bennett

Yorkshire Terriers
Dog Books for Kids
K. Bennett

Dogs
Top Ten Dog Breeds For Kids
Amazing Animal Books For Young Readers
Zahra Jazael & John Davidson

Cats For Kids
Amazing Animal Books For Young Readers
K. Bennett & John Davidson

Foxes For Kids
Amazing Animal Books For Young Readers
Zahra Jazael & John Davidson

Wolves For Kids
Amazing Animal Books For Young Readers
By John Davidson and Virginia Fidler

www.ingramcontent.com/pod-product-compliance
Lightning Source LLC
Chambersburg PA
CBHW040317010626
45792CB00022B/701